The Kingfisher

This year the winter is very cold,
with ice and snow everywhere.
Some wild animals and birds
are finding it hard to survive.
Kim the kingfisher sits on a branch
in his place above his favourite stream.
He can no longer dive for fish, because
thick ice has covered the surface of the water.

Kim the kingfisher is aching with hunger.
He flies slowly away from his stream
in search of some open water.
If he does not find food within a few hours,
he will die of hunger and cold.
At last he comes to a frozen pond.
Someone has made a hole in the ice.
For a few moments, Kim hovers above this hole.
Then he dives into the icy water,
and catches a small silver fish.

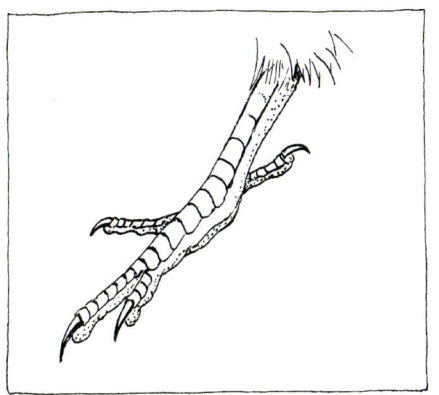 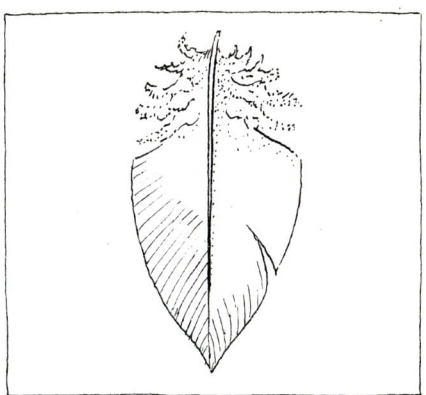

Spring has returned to the stream at last.
The leaves are growing on the trees.
Kim sits on his usual branch, looking down
at his handsome reflection in the water.
People say that the kingfisher is in love
with himself, as he looks at his image.
But Kim is not admiring his bright plumage.
He is waiting for a fish to swim past.
Then he will dive, as swift as an arrow,
and come up with a catch in his long beak.

A female kingfisher flies past.
Kim calls to her: "Chee, kee . . ."
With a flash of blue wings, she turns in the air,
and flies back towards Kim's tree. For a while,
Kim chases her away from his territory.
But at last he allows her to sit beside him.
She sees that his stream is a good place to fish.
Her search for a mate is over.

The two kingfishers take turns
at digging a tunnel in the bank.
They peck the earth with their beaks
and scoop out soil with their claws.
The tunnel is about one metre long.
It has a round space at the far end.

A month later, the tunnel is finished.
Now the two birds go through a special courtship.
The female kingfisher opens her beak,
like a young chick begging its parent for food.
In no time at all, Kim catches a fish.
He tosses it in the air, and gives it to his mate
head-first, ready for her to swallow.
Now the female kingfisher can tell that Kim
will be a good provider for his family.

The kingfishers mate in the bulrushes.
For the next few days, they fly together,
one behind the other, low over the stream.
Kim's mate lays seven round white eggs
in the small space at the end of the tunnel.
The eggs are laid on the bare earth
among a litter of fishbones.
Both parents take turns at keeping the eggs warm.
They sit and cover them with their wings.

About three weeks later, the eggs begin to hatch.
Each new-born baby bird has no feathers.
It sits on the bare, dark floor
among the fishbones which litter the nest.
It waits for one of its parents to come.
Soon Kim and his mate are busy all day long,
bringing food for their seven new chicks.

Young kingfishers eat insects, grubs and small fish,
which their parents bring down the tunnel.
The baby birds are always hungry.
They grow quickly during the next few days.
The two parents work hard from dawn till dusk.

A kingfisher's nest is not lined with moss or down,
like the nests which birds build above ground.
The floor of the tunnel becomes covered in fishbones,
which the parents and chicks bring up after eating.
Within a few days, it has a strong, fishy smell.

The hungriest chick sits near the entrance.
When it has been fed, it moves back
so that the next chick can take its place.
Each young bird gets its fair share
of the food which the busy parents provide.
After about two weeks, the young kingfishers
grow quills from which their feathers will open out.
These quills protect the feathers from the dirt
which lies on the floor of the nest.

A month has gone by since the chicks hatched.
It is a calm day in summer.
Kim's mate sits on a branch and calls:
"Chee, kee..." The boldest young bird
comes to the tunnel entrance and looks out.
Its feathers have now come through the quills.
It is ready at last to fly.
The fledgeling flutters up to the branch,
and sits beside its mother in the sunshine.

Within a short time, all the young birds are fledged.
They leave the tunnel with its dark, smelly nest.
They dive and chase the silver, darting fish.
For several days their parents will still feed them.
But when they can fish for themselves, the parents
will chase them away to find territories of their own.

Some facts about kingfishers

Kim is an ordinary European kingfisher.
He lives beside rivers, slow-moving streams,
lakes, canals, and ponds where fish are found.
Kingfishers eat insects, and sometimes frogs.
But, as their name says, they prefer to eat fish.
Kingfishers are found throughout the world,
in tropical forests, and by cool northern streams.
The enemies of the kingfisher are rats,
stoats, and weasels, who sometimes rob its nest.
Storms and floods can also damage the tunnel.
But nowadays, the main enemy of the kingfisher
is the pollution which affects streams and rivers,
so that fish cannot survive in them.
There are many legends about the bright kingfisher.
The Greeks called him 'Halcyon', the bird
of fair weather and calm seas.

Racket-tailed kingfisher
(New Guinea)

Giant kingfisher
(Tropical Africa)

Belted kingfisher
(North America)

Texas or green kingfisher
(North and South America)

Small three-toed
kingfisher (Asia and
Australasia)